HISTORIC PHOTOS OF
RENO

TEXT AND CAPTIONS BY DONNELYN CURTIS

TURNER
PUBLISHING COMPANY

Virginia Street, in the heart of the business district, toward the north from the Truckee River in the early 1920s. The post office is on the right.

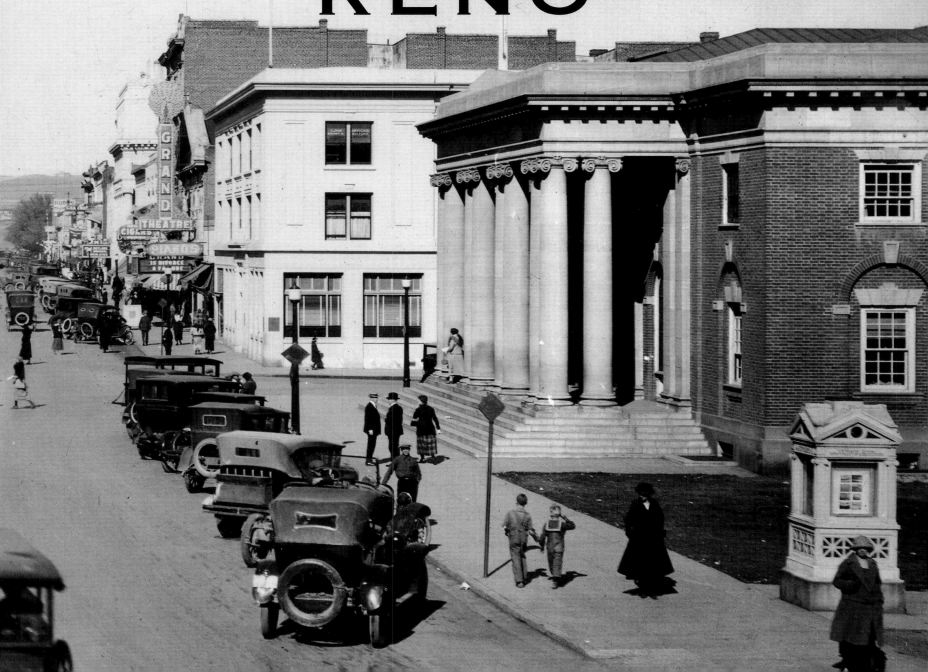

HISTORIC PHOTOS OF
RENO

Turner Publishing Company
200 4th Avenue North • Suite 950
Nashville, Tennessee 37219
(615) 255-2665

www.turnerpublishing.com

Historic Photos of Reno

Copyright © 2008 Turner Publishing Company

Library of Congress Control Number: 2007942092

ISBN-13: 978-1-59652-438-5

Printed in the United States of America

08 09 10 11 12 13 14 15—0 9 8 7 6 5 4 3 2 1

Contents

A view of Reno taken to the southwest from the University of Nevada (ca. 1898).

Acknowledgments

This volume, *Historic Photos of Reno,* is the result of the cooperation and efforts of many individuals, organizations, and corporations. It is with great thanks that we acknowledge the valuable contribution of the following for their generous support:

Library of Congress
University of Nevada, Special Collections
Shane Anderson

We would also like to thank the following individuals for valuable contributions and assistance in making this work possible:

Kathryn Totton, Photo Archivist in Special Collections at the University of Nevada, Reno Libraries and an expert on Nevada history
James Bantin, University Archivist in Special Collections at the University of Nevada, Reno Libraries
Melissa Rivera, the student assistant in Special Collections who digitized most of the photographs
Dr. James Herz, the avid collector and generous donor of the majority of the photos in this book, whose own research efforts provided important clues to the stories of the photos
Dr. Anton Sohn of the University of Nevada School of Medicine, for sharing his History of Medicine in Nevada photos
The many photographers who documented Reno's history so beautifully, and the many donors who lovingly preserved and generously provided the photographs to Special Collections

PREFACE

Reno has always been a colorful city in an unconventional state. Conversely, the majority of the population has led conventional lives outside of the neon corridor. Several novelists and historians have observed that Reno is full of parallel universes. Photographers have documented the orderly development of a western metropolis, as well as some of the aspects that have earned Reno its sometimes scandalous reputation. Taken as a whole, the photographs in this book illustrate the multi-faceted character of "The Biggest Little City in the World."

The intent of this book is to let photographs speak for themselves in presenting the history of Reno, with minimal interpretation. In selecting the images, our researchers have made every effort to portray a broad and comprehensive view of the city's past. We have painstakingly probed the corners of photo archives to uncover depictions of the lesser-known, the surprising, and the unique aspects of the history of Reno.

The photographs are presented in approximate chronological order, grouped together within eras of Reno's history. Short introductions describe the eras to provide historical context. The captions add details about the individual photos to help readers understand the times, places, and circumstances depicted. Most of the photographs in the book were selected from the rich photo archives of Special Collections at the University of Nevada, Reno Library.

With the exception of touching up imperfections caused by the passage of time and cropping where necessary, no other changes have been made. The focus and clarity of the images is limited to the tools and the abilities of the photographers at the times they were taken. On behalf of future historians, the author urges readers to label their treasured photographs! The people, locations, times, and events portrayed in your photo album might be familiar to you, but fifty years after your demise, those facts may be lost forever.

The photographs in the first section cover Reno's early history, from 1868 through 1909. The second section explores the time period 1910–1929, when Reno was developing its personality (or rather, multiple personalities). Section Three, 1930–1949, documents a period of adjusting to new economic conditions and new approaches to economic development. Section Four, 1950–1979, covers Reno's further growth and maturation. In each of these sections we have attempted to capture the many facets of Reno's personality.

Through this project, the author has developed a heightened appreciation and gratitude for the work of historians who have previously done such meticulous research on Reno's history, without the benefits of contemporary online tools.

We encourage readers to view contemporary Reno with these historic images in mind. How can we protect and preserve the fragments of the past that help us understand the present and plan for the future? Photographs preserve the past and provide pleasure, but they can serve another purpose as well: they can help us discern the remnants of earlier times that are still with us—though sometimes overshadowed—within our present environment.

Construction of the Central Pacific Railroad tracks along the Truckee
River east of Reno. The railroad stop in Reno triggered the town's
permanent settlement.

HUB OF THE MINING BOOMS

(1868–1909)

The location that would become Reno had no permanent residents until the middle of the nineteenth century. The Native Americans in the area were nomadic. European-American explorers mapped and described the area in the 1830s and 1840s, and California-bound immigrants first stopped in the Truckee Meadows in 1841.

Nevada owes much of its earliest development to rich lodes of gold and silver, and mining has played an important role in the economic history of Reno. The site was first a staging area for California gold seekers after their trek across the Great Basin and before they faced the rigors of the Sierra Nevada Mountains.

After 1859, when gold was discovered in Nevada 25 miles to the southeast of the Truckee River wagon stop, traffic began to flow in the other direction. When the richer Comstock silver lode was discovered in 1861, the "Rush to Washoe" was huge. The enterprising Myron Lake purchased Charles Fuller's Truckee River toll bridge, on the route from Donner Pass to the Comstock. He then built a hotel and began acquiring land.

Lake's crossing was always a busy stop for travelers and for the lumber and ranching trades and other suppliers that built and sustained Virginia City and the mines. But it was Myron Lake's success in securing a Central Pacific Railroad stop that secured Reno's destiny as a railroad town and regional center that would outlive the mining boom.

He gave the Central Pacific 40 acres to establish a depot and a community. In 1868 the railroad auctioned 400 lots, and 100 homes and businesses were established within a month. The settlement was named for Jesse Reno, a Union general killed in the Civil War. Reno became the Washoe County seat in 1871 and was incorporated in 1876 but was without a city government until 1903. The state university was moved from Elko to Reno in 1885, and commerce continued to flourish despite the fact that Comstock mining declined and Virginia City fell into a depression by 1880. The transportation industry provided a stable economic base, and Reno served as a hub for a large area.

Its population was 4,500 at the turn of the century. That doubled in the next decade after gold and silver were discovered in 1900 in Tonopah and Goldfield. Roads to the new lodes passed through Reno, which once again supplied mines and miners with goods and services.

Freight wagons, men, and teams of the Sierra Nevada Transport Company on a road through the snow in the Donner Pass of the Sierra Nevada Mountains in early spring (ca. 1896).

A view of Six-Mile Canyon from C Street in Virginia City in 1865, when Reno was little more than a river crossing. Proximity to this larger town aided Reno's growth as a transportation hub and, after the 1880 depression, it surpassed the declining Virginia City.

Engine #11, *Reno,* of the Virginia and Truckee Railroad at a roundhouse in Reno in the late 1800s. The V&T, the "crookedest short line in America" connected Virginia City with the Central Pacific Railroad in Reno in 1879. In the beginning, 36 trains a day carried passengers and freight. Lumber from Carson Valley mills and supplies were transported to Virginia City, and ore was hauled on the return runs to Reno.

A rather quiet day at the Reno railroad yard. In 1885, the Central Pacific line was leased to the Southern Pacific Railroad.

Myron Lake's hotel and the first steel bridge across the Truckee River, about 1883, at the corner of Sierra and Third Streets. The first Washoe County Courthouse is in the background.

A photographer facing east along the Truckee River shot this early
image of Reno.

A fire at the Palace Club, the largest gambling house in the state, attracted a large crowd.
There were no restrictions on gambling in Reno until 1910. The railroad depot is in the
background.

A blacksmith shop on Center Street, 1893. The two men in the center are identified as Baldwin and S. E. Cooper, a blacksmith. The Golden Hotel was built on this site in 1906. A fire in 1962 destroyed the Golden Hotel and killed six people. The 24-story hotel that was rebuilt in 1963 was purchased by Bill Harrah three years later and became part of Harrah's.

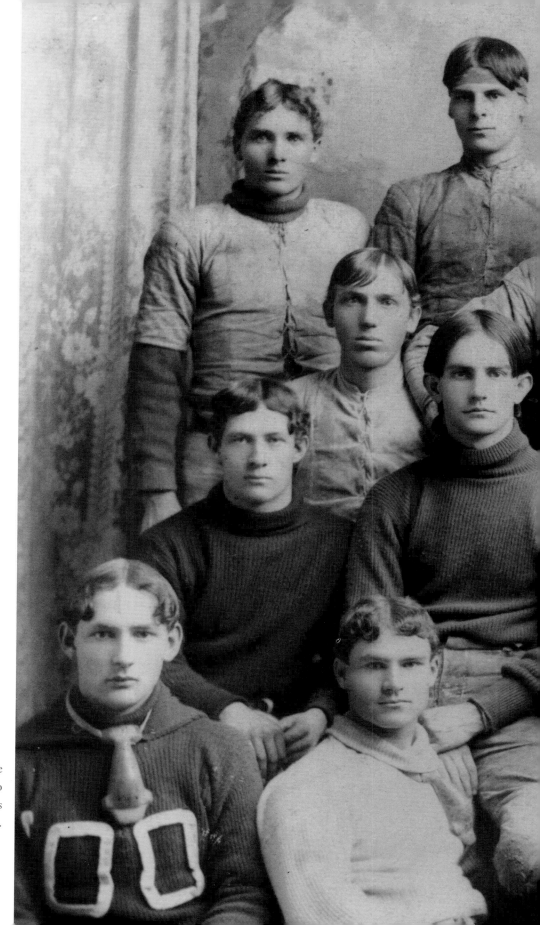

The football team of the University of Nevada, 1896. The university was founded in 1874 in Elko and moved to Reno in 1887. For 75 years the university was Nevada's only institution of higher education.

The interior of an unidentified bar in Reno in the 1800s.

The house staff of the Nevada Hospital for Mental Disease, which opened in 1882 (ca.1890).
Patients did agricultural work on the property, which eventually housed the university farm.

The Fulton house was built in Virginia City in 1875 and later abandoned when fortunes changed. It was purchased, dismantled, moved to Reno and reassembled on the bank of the Truckee River on West First Street in 1884 by Robert Fulton, the owner of the *Reno Gazette* newspaper. The property later became the Reno city park that is directly across the river from Trinity Episcopal Church.

14

Employees in front of the Reno Cash Store at 315 Virginia, established as a grocery and general merchandise store in 1903 by Robert Nelson, a city councilman. Ross Peterson was an early partner until 1915. The name of the store was later changed to the California Market. It closed in 1959.

A streetcar on the Virginia Street bridge over the Truckee River around 1903. The Masonic Building is under construction.

A butcher's delivery wagon in front of Smith's Cash Store at 129
Virginia Street around 1904. Half the store was a butcher shop, and for
several years it served as the only retail butcher outlet.

The entrance to the University of Nevada, Reno, around 1900. Hatch Hall, originally the State Mining Laboratory, is on the right. On the left is Morrill Hall, the first building on campus (still standing and in use), built in 1886 and named for the Vermont Senator, Justin Morrill, who was the author of the land-grant act establishing the university.

The interior of a bar in the nearby town of Sparks, showing
a slot machine in the background. Sparks, now contiguous
with Reno, was established in 1904 when the Southern Pacific
Railroad moved its switch yard and maintenance buildings,
along with the houses for workers, to the area. The town was
named for John Sparks, the governor of Nevada at the time.
The estimated population of Sparks in 2005 was 82,051.

Teamsters haul logs from the Tahoe area in the early 1900s. The fast-growing town depended on lumber brought in from the nearby mountain forests.

A wooden flume along the Truckee River. Flumes channeled water from the river to power plants that provided electricity for Reno's industrial and residential growth.

Sierra logs await processing in the pond of the Verdi Lumber Company sawmill, located 15 miles to the west of Reno, around 1904.

The John Newton Evans house in 1905, at the south edge of what would become the University of Nevada, Reno. Evans, a prominent banker, was instrumental in relocating the university from Elko to Reno, selling the land upon which the campus was built. In 1925 the house on Evans Avenue was sold to the Sigma Alpha Epsilon fraternity. It was later replaced by another building. The adjacent Evans property became a city park.

The Reno High School girls' basketball team. On the top row, left to right, are Rowena Evans, Dora Rice, Edith Fransden, Coach Bess Evans, Ethel Brown, and Ethel Thompson. On the bottom row are Leola Lewis, Grace Mahon, Schadler (first name unknown), and Lela White.

The Reno Amusement Company, Aetna Skating Rink, and the Southern Nevada
Wagon Company buggy and tack dealership at the corner of Fourth and Sierra.

A horse and wagon in Reno's commercial district in the early 1900s.

The Moana Baths at Moana Hot Springs. A streetcar line built in 1907 transported bathers from downtown Reno to the spa, which opened as a resort in 1905, with a small lake and boating facilities as well as a baseball field and a large, indoor swimming pool.

The interior of an unidentified grocery store in Reno, stocked with boxes of Sunny Monday laundry soap and Royal Swastika brand sodas from American Biscuit Company. The swastika was an honored symbol among Native American tribes long before Nazi Germany corrupted its meaning.

During the many years of unregulated open grazing, it was necessary for ranchers to protect their water supplies from itinerant herds, as well as wild horses. Once open grazing became regulated and much more limited, fencing was needed to contain ranch livestock. The sign inside promotes fencing for lawns and cemeteries as well.

The funeral of General Orlando Evans, the oldest of the Evans brothers, at the house of his brother, John Newton Evans, 835 Evans Avenue.

Following Spread: Reno policemen.

Patrick Flanigan was a highly successful sheep rancher in Nevada and California. He was the first sheepman in Nevada to ship wool directly to Chicago and Kansas City from the Flanigan Warehouse in Reno on East Fourth Street. His Nevada Packing Company processed large quantities of meat from area ranchers. Flanigan was instrumental in producing electric power for the area and was active in Nevada politics.

A Southern Pacific Railroad work crew poses with heavy equipment. Reno's role as a railroad hub kept its economy relatively stable as mining waned.

38

Clearing snow from the Southern Pacific railroad tracks in the Sierra Nevada between Reno and Sacramento could be a monumental job.

The statue of John Mackay, a silver
baron of Virginia City, in front of
the Mackay School of Mines on
the quadrangle at the University
of Nevada, Reno. The statue and
building were financed by the Mackay
family and dedicated to the university
on June 10, 1908.

Gutzon Borglum and his wife in their later years. The sculptor was commissioned to make the John Mackay statue, and also to carve Mount Rushmore.

The day of the Jack Johnson–Jim Jeffries fight in Reno, July 4, 1910. The event was the most famous prizefight of the time. It exacerbated racial tensions across America and focused the country's attention on Reno.

EMERGING PLAYGROUND

(1910–1929)

Reno's next two decades were lively in several ways. While most of Reno's established townspeople lived typical western American lives—raising their children; building businesses, schools, churches, parks, and a library; forming civic, fraternal and arts organizations and participating in Fourth of July parades and picnics—a significant transient population was nourishing and promoting different kinds of culture.

Members of a thriving divorce colony, attracted by the state's liberal divorce laws, bolstered Reno's economy, exerted cosmopolitan influences on the city for the next several decades, and kept tabloid journalists busy.

Reno, as a railroad and freighting town and the regional center for mining and ranching, served the needs and desires of young men out on the town. Reno was known regionally, if not nationally, as Nevada's "sin city" long before Las Vegas sprang up in the south. Reno's unregulated gambling, drinking and prostitution generated the city's first tourist trade, and special events attracted more tourists. Gambling continued underground after it was outlawed in 1910, and Prohibition was not successful. In fact, several Renoites made a good living in the rum-running business. Gambling was coupled with money-laundering, and Reno was known to harbor notorious gangsters.

Reno's "fight of the century," the heavyweight championship in 1910 between Jack Johnson and Jim Jeffries, temporarily tripled the population, and the value of entertainment and good times became apparent. The theaters featured actors and performers from San Francisco and New York, and hot springs resorts and nearby Lake Tahoe offered recreational opportunities for both tourists and locals. For a town its size, Reno had a lot going on.

The Reno Rodeo, first held in 1919, attracted large crowds for several days each year. The Transcontinental Highways Exposition in 1927 celebrated the completion of the Lincoln Highway and the Victory Highway that directed cross-country automobile and trucking traffic through town.

Naturally, there was tension between those who believed Reno should become more respectable and those who recognized the economic benefits of a permissive environment. Reform attempts were sometimes successful but only temporarily. When the legislature changed the mandatory residency requirement for divorce from six months to a year in 1913, the impact on Reno's economy was so dramatic that the 1915 legislature changed the requirement back to six months. A prevailing philosophy favored minimal regulation and lax enforcement in areas of personal choice.

A group of Paiute Indians gambling on a street in Reno in 1910.

The Johnson–Jeffries Fight, held July 4, 1910, was called the Fight of the Century. After San Francisco canceled the fight between Jack Johnson, the first black heavyweight champion of the world, and Jim Jeffries, a former champion, Reno had two weeks to build a stadium and prepare for the more than 22,000 spectators who attended the match.

Jeffries, the "Great White Hope," had the crowd behind him. Few approved of Johnson's relations with white women or his flamboyance. Jeffries came out of retirement for this occasion, never having lost a fight, but he was unable to make a comeback, and withdrew from the fight after 15 rounds.

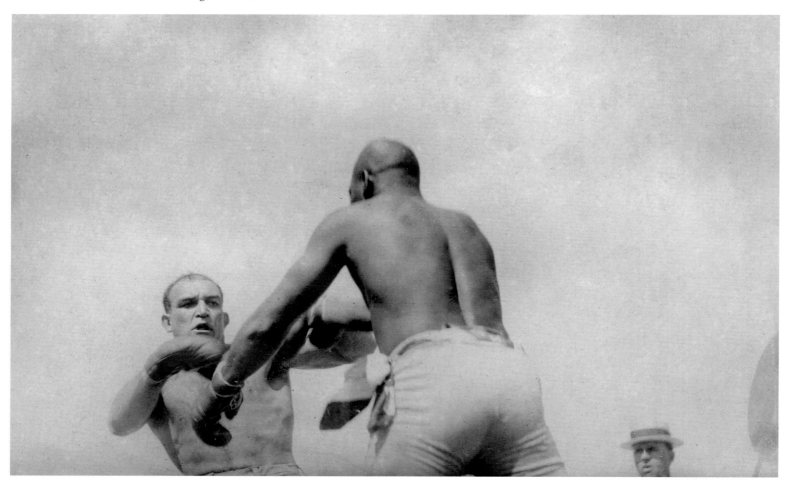

The outcome of the fight triggered riots all over the country, as angry white people clashed with blacks who were celebrating the victory. The racism unleashed by this event was a shock to many.

Looking down on a crowded bar in the Louvre casino on "The last night of open gambling in Reno, 1910" (October 8). Prior to the legislative ban of 1910, gambling in Nevada had few restrictions. From 1910 until 1931, when it was again legalized, undercover gambling persisted on a smaller scale.

A game of faro in a Reno casino, October 8, 1910.

Chism Ice Cream wagons, 1912. Edward Chism established the ice creamery in 1905, while his brother John ran the Chism Dairy (later the Crescent Dairy) from 1900 until the 1950s. By 1904, the family owned the largest number of milk cows in the State of Nevada. After buying the ice cream company in 1960, Carnation continued to use the Chism name locally until the 1970s.

A Reno Fire Department wagon (ca. 1912).

A float in the suffrage parade in the summer of 1914, with the theme "Nevada, Don't Keep Your Women Out!" The float, which was awarded the $25 second prize, represents "Nevada standing at the gate waiting to be admitted to her free sisters." It is sitting in front of the courthouse.

Anne Martin and Mabel Vernon campaigning for women's suffrage in their automobile in 1914.

Harvesting potatoes in rural Sparks at the Cappuro farm. Italian immigrants became prominent land owners in the Reno area.

A biplane landing in a field in Reno around 1915. The city didn't have an airfield until 1920. Airmail service was implemented in 1921, and the first commercial airline began its operations in Reno in 1927.

Another view of the biplane, skimming above the fields.

The Sierra Grotto-Mazetti bar's interior.

Manzanita Lake at the University of Nevada, viewed to the north.

Following Spread: Shriners marching on Mackay
Field at the University of Nevada.

A parade in Reno, with World War I soldiers.

The Woman's Relief Corps marching in a parade, with Mrs. John N. Evans in the lead. The WRC was a patriotic auxiliary organization to the Grand Army of the Republic, which was comprised of veterans of the Union Army in the Civil War.

Raymond I. "Pappy" Smith, the patriarch of Reno's spectacularly successful casino Harolds Club, in his early days when he was making a living running games of chance at county fairs.

The Truckee River and Virginia Street bridge in the 1920s.

A ranch scene along the
Reno-Carson Highway, now
Highway 395.

67

A view of the Riverside Bridge at Booth Street under construction, with steel reinforcing rods in place, July 1920.

An aerial photo of Reno in 1922, at Commercial Row and Virginia Street, looking southeast. The railroad depot and train tracks are in the center.

Tony Pecetti's jazz band (Tony is playing the accordion), 1920.

Donner Lake Memorial Bridge on Highway 40, under construction in 1925 with Donner Lake in the background. The ill-fated Donner Party blazed this major route through the northern Sierra Nevada in the winter of 1846–47. Trapped by a severe winter storm, over half of them died and many resorted to cannibalism to survive.

A Reno family ready for a swim in the 1920s.

This German Big Bertha howitzer came through Reno mounted on a train car after World War I.

University of Nevada students outside the first Education Building (now the Thompson Building).

Young women on an automobile on the university campus.

The indoor swimming pool at Moana Hot Springs.

Directors and employees of the Washoe County Bank at Virginia and Second Street, June 18, 1921.

A group of people, mainly children, in front of Majestic Theater in 1925.

The cast of a children's play, *One Night in a Nursery*, in the Majestic Theater around 1923. The Majestic was built in 1910 with 1,216 seats, joining the Wheelman's Theater and McKissick Opera House. Later, the Granada Theater was added to the group that attracted top-name entertainers to the city. By 1920, these large theaters were featuring movies as well as live performances.

The Wigwam movie theater, showcasing a stage coach used in *The Iron Horse,* the first major film directed by John Ford, which was largely filmed in Wadsworth, near Reno, in 1924.

Reno Elks Club Luncheon at the Al Tahoe Inn in honor of Grand Exalted
Ruler of the B.P.O.E., W. H. Atwell, in July 1925.

Reno Evening Gazette building, South Virginia Street, Reno (ca. 1927).

The Federal Outfitting
Company clothing store
on Sierra Street was
offering free bridge lamps
as a promotion around
1928.

Installing a sign for the
Federal Outfitting Company,
which opened in 1928.

University of Nevada drama students in costume.

The Dodge Brothers dealership and garage, around 1927. By the mid-1920s, there were 12 automobile dealerships in Reno.

The Riverside Cigar Store in the Riverside Hotel in Reno (ca. 1927). The location of the
Riverside Hotel is on the exact site of the Lake House hotel, the first building in Reno.

The traveling Home Canning truck of the Kerr Glass
Manufacturing Corporation (ca. 1927).

An auto barge makes its way across Lake Tahoe. Only 28 miles from
Reno, the spectacular lake was a favorite getaway for local residents.
Its proximity also brought tourist dollars to Reno.

Nevada Sporting Goods store, on the northwest corner of Douglas Alley and Virginia Street, around 1927. Hunting, fishing, and outdoor recreation were always popular in the Reno area.

A Sierra Dray Line truck (ca. 1927).

Virginia Street, viewed to the north from First Street.

A parade marching south on Virginia Street past the Grand Central and
St. Frances hotels.

A Reno department store interior with employees (ca. 1927).

Christmas tree lighting ceremony with Reno dignitaries in their organizational regalia.

These YMCA boys were photographed at the Century Club on West First Street at Christmastime.

Native Americans in a parade on East First Street, passing Truckee River Power Company, Fraley's clothing store, and the YWCA. This appears to have been a promotion for the 1925 movie *The Vanishing American,* based on a novel by Zane Gray.

A parade on Sierra Street, near First Street. The
Parkway Hotel was built in 1925.

A parade in front of the Colonial Apartments (later called Ross Manor) on
First and West streets in downtown Reno.

The Truckee River flooded on March 25, 1928. Boys were catching fish
in the streets after attempted barricades failed to contain the water.

The Truckee River flood at the Virginia Street bridge.

Some of the damage to Wingfield Park caused by the 1928 flood.

Burke & Short Men's Clothing store on Virginia Street, which later
became the Herd & Short store.

The State Building in Powning Park, around 1927. It was built for the Transcontinental Highways Exposition and later turned over to Washoe County.

Firefighters respond to a fire in the building housing Grandma's Doughnuts, Coffee, and Waffles shop.

The Piggly Wiggly Grocery Store on Sierra Street in downtown Reno.

A store window of the Golden Rule Mercantile Company on Sierra Street displays toy animals for 49¢ and a train set for under $9. In 1928, the shop became a J. C. Penney store.

A tow truck from the 3A Garage in Reno, a distributor of Samson Cords tires.

The Rifle Team at the
University of Nevada, 1926.

Laying the cornerstone for the First Methodist Church at First
and West streets in 1926.

Louis Rosasco (standing behind the accordian) and his jazz band.

Following Spread: An airmail plane in front of the Reno
Aerial Mail hangar at the new airfield. Mail flights landed
in Reno daily.

The Fokker Trimotor airplane that Richard Byrd flew on his North Pole expedition stopped by the Reno airport November 1, 1926, during a tour of 40 U.S. cities.

A parade honoring Charles A. Lindbergh, who is in the lead car with
Reno's mayor E. E. Roberts, September 19, 1927.

A publicity photo for the Transcontinental Highways Exposition in Reno. The exposition was planned for 1926 but was delayed until 1927.

A booster delegation for the Transcontinental Highways Exposition in Reno, 1927. The exposition celebrated the completion of the Victory Highway and also the Lincoln Highway, the first coast-to-coast route. Both highways shared the same road from Wadsworth to Sacramento through Reno, which recognized the benefit of the traffic.

A publicity event on the Nevada/California state line, promoting the Transcontinental Highways Exposition. Reno had great hopes for economic gain from the event, but it was less successful than hoped and incurred a deficit in Washoe County funds that required a special tax levy.

A cabin thought to have been occupied by author Mark Twain was brought to Idlewild Park for exhibit in 1927. Twain, whose real name was Samuel L. Clemens, came to Nevada with his brother Orion, who had been appointed secretary of the Nevada Territory by President Abraham Lincoln. Failing as a silver prospector, Sam first used the name Mark Twain in 1863 while writing for the *Territorial Enterprise* newspaper in Virginia City. In 1864, he moved to San Francisco.

The Victor Talking Machine Company exhibit at the Transcontinental
Highways Exposition at Idlewild Park in 1927 was next to a booth promoting
Carnation canned milk and Fluff cake flour.

One of the carnival rides, the Whip, at the Transcontinental Highways Exposition.

The first Reno Arch was erected on Virginia Street to advertise the exposition.
Dedicated on October 23, 1926, it was lit every night for ten months.

After the exposition, a prize of $100 was offered for a permanent motto to be mounted on the empty arch. "The Biggest Little City in the World" was the winning entry, and the slogan is still in use on the latest arch, an enduring Reno icon.

The "New Easy washer with the marvelous new clothes dryer" on display
in front of the Truckee River Power Company offices.

The J. C. Penney store on Sierra Street.

Following Spread: Machinists inside a Southern Pacific
Railroad shop in Sparks, around 1927.

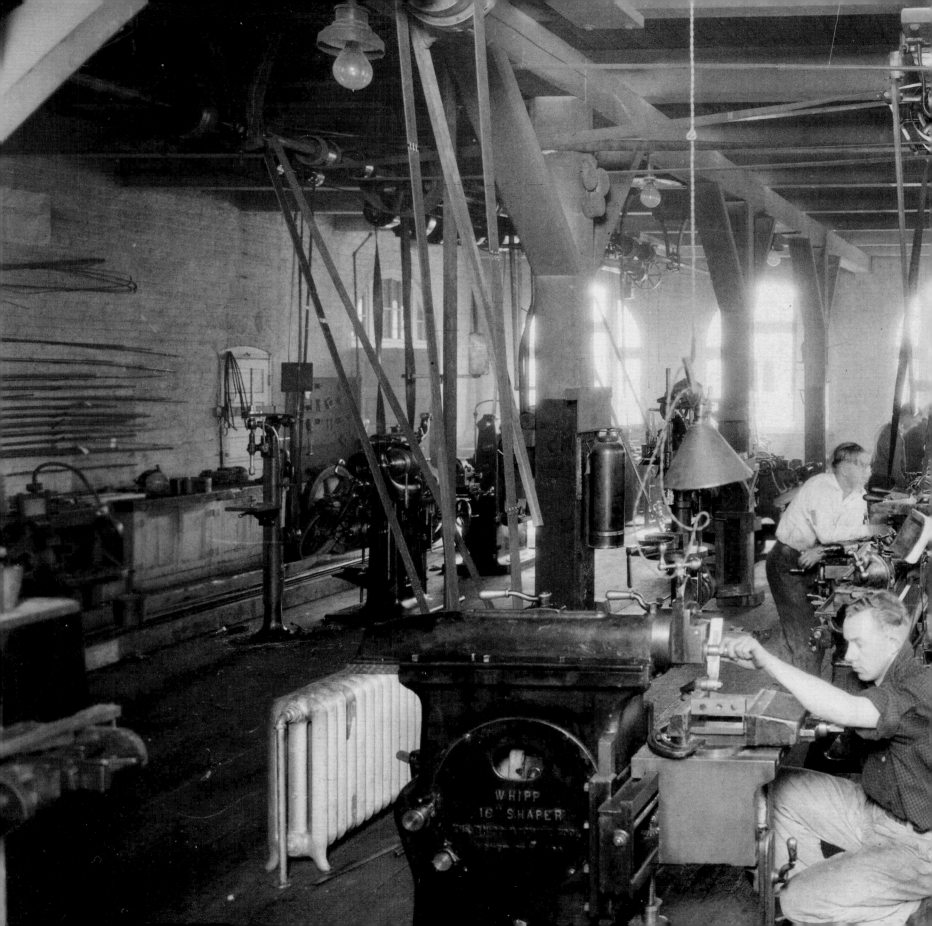

The racetrack at the Washoe County Fairgrounds in Reno. The Humphrey Supply Company Building in the background, a meat packing plant, was designed by Frederic DeLongchamps.

Inside the KOH radio station, April 1929. KOH began broadcasting in Reno on October 27, 1928, and still operates today.

The Bank Club on Center Street operated illegally in a basement until gambling was legalized in 1931. At that time, it expanded into a ground-floor space, becoming the largest casino licensed in the state. This photo shows the co-owner, James McKay, who was later sent to prison for mail fraud. It was widely known that McKay and his partner Bill Graham were involved in a number of nefarious activities including money laundering, harboring gangland fugitives, and prostitution.

NEW APPROACHES TO ECONOMIC DEVELOPMENT

(1930–1949)

The stock market crash of 1929 hurt Reno—most of the banks closed and the fortune of George Wingfield, Nevada's wealthy political kingpin, was wiped out in 1932—but the city's unconventional economy was able to limp through the Great Depression. To stimulate the economy, the legislature legalized gambling once again in 1931. The 1927 legislature had reduced the residency requirement for divorce to three months, and in 1931 it was further reduced to six weeks. Reno began to advertise itself as a divorce destination, and that year there were more than 4,000 divorce-seekers in the area. The new Riverside Hotel was full, and dude ranches on the outskirts of the city were thriving.

A related industry came to town: wedding chapels. California had a waiting period for marriages and later required medical tests. In contrast, local judges made it easy to have an impulse wedding. Thousands of couples eloped to Reno every year.

Prizefighting also attracted tourists during the 1930s. Prominent boxers and their celebrity friends frequented Reno. The climate was favorable for outdoor boxing, horse racing, golfing, and similar attractions. Savvy promoters staged and publicized numerous celebrity events.

Nevada's tax laws were favorable to the wealthy, and Norman Biltz, an enterprising real estate developer, made sure that multimillionaires were aware of that fact. He lured dozens of them to Lake Tahoe, becoming quite wealthy himself. Reno arts and the University of Nevada garnered philanthropic benefits from transplanted benefactors such as E. L. Cord and Max Fleischmann.

Even though gambling was legalized, gambling houses at first kept a low profile. Not much changed visibly until two entrepreneurial outsiders showed up. Harold Smith bought a small casino, and later went into partnership with his father, Raymond I. "Pappy" Smith, and his brother Raymond, Jr. The Smiths did something very different in advertising their casino. "Harolds Club or Bust" billboards and road signs appeared all over the world. Bill Harrah was another Reno newcomer who started small, with a bingo parlor, and built an empire. Neon, combination hotel-casinos, and big-name casino entertainers had arrived. Slot machines began to appear in grocery stores and laundromats. Fewer men were around during the war, and women took on new roles working as dealers and croupiers.

This view to the east on First Street shows the elegant Deauville Casino Cabaret at the corner of First and West. The Deauville was open for only a few months in 1931 before its owners declared bankruptcy.

Interior of the Northern Club casino in the Commercial Hotel on Center Street. Gambling was legalized in Nevada in 1931, and in 1933 the Northern Club was licensed for ten table games and three slot machines.

The updated Reno arch on Virginia Street. Neon was added to the sign in 1934.

A typical university professor's house, at 245 University Terrace, January 1930. Jay Carpenter, a professor of mining engineering, lived here when he was the chair of the Mackay School of Mines.

University of Nevada, Reno students and faculty on the lawn in front of
the Mackay School of Mines prior to a field expedition.

"Ye Old News Stand" in downtown Reno was displaying wanted posters and newspaper stories as part of a promotion for its selection of detective magazines when this photo was snapped.

The Southern Pacific Railroad depot.

A Southern Pacific Giant 5000 engine at the Reno station in the 1930s.

Jack Dempsey built a boxing ring known as Dempsey's Bowl near the racetrack while he was in town for a rest and a divorce in 1931. Celebrities posed for a photograph there prior to the July 4, 1932, match between Max Baer and King Levinsky. From the left are: the fight announcer, Wallace Beery; the wealthy political boss, George Wingfield; Lieutenant Governor Morley Griswold; Jim Tully; an unidentified man; Leonard Sacks (Jack Dempsey's manager); Dempsey; Governor Frederick Balzar; and actor Tom Mix. Max Baer won the fight in a 20-round decision.

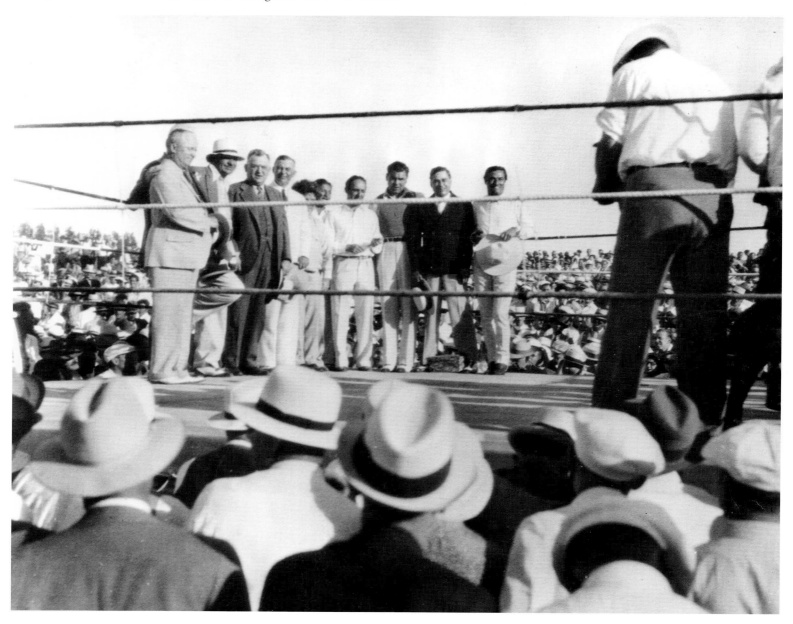

An operating room in St. Mary's Hospital in the 1930s. The hospital was established by Dominican sisters in 1908. The nurses' training school established in St. Mary's in 1910 was incorporated into the nursing program at the University of Neveada in 1959.

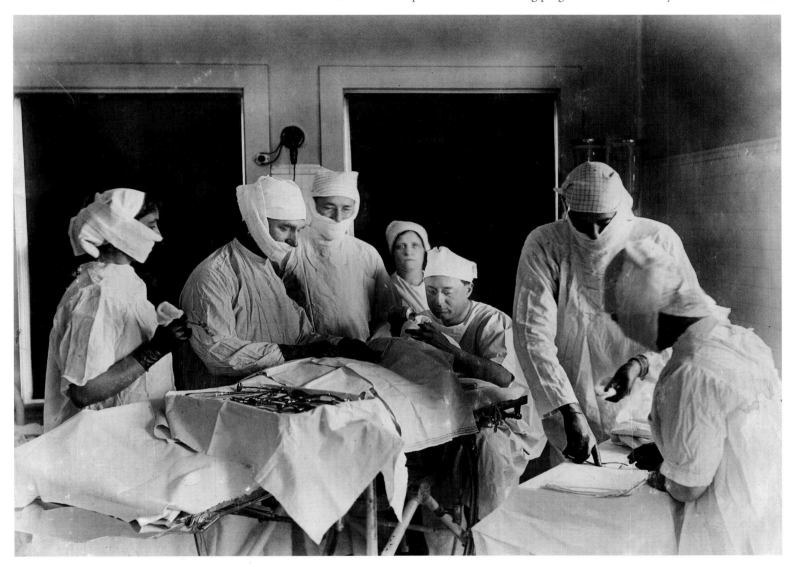

Douglas Alley in downtown Reno. Casinos and clubs were packed tightly into the central "red zone," inside boundaries drawn in red on the map of Reno and strictly maintained by city officials for more than two decades.

The Reno post office, designed by Frederic DeLongchamps in the zigzag moderne style. The building opened in 1934 and is still in use.

A skier from the
University of Nevada
ski team at Mt. Rose
(ca. 1937).

One of Reno's larger theaters, the Granada, in 1938. Theaters and casinos were able to maintain house bands and orchestras and stage extravagant shows with guest celebrities.

Center Street, inside Reno's red zone, was packed with passenger cars, but a taxi stand and the
Pacific Stage Greyhound bus depot (right) offered additional transport for out-of-towners.

North Virginia Street at night, around 1940.

Manzanita Lake and
Manzanita Hall at
the University of
Nevada, Reno, 1940.

Feeding ducks in Idlewild Park, 1940.

Cave Rock tunnel at Lake Tahoe (ca. 1940s).

Murray's Cocktail Lounge
in the 1940s.

Postal workers in front of the Reno Post Office.

The shantytown along the Truckee River, 1944.

Harold Smith and Raymond I. "Pappy" Smith, the proprietors of Harolds Club, with George Southworth, a Reno businessman and politician, in front of the casino.

A Union Pacific train outside of Reno in 1944.

The Riverside Hotel was the tallest building in Reno for several years, and its sign was visible from miles away.

The Truckee River in downtown Reno. Spires of the St. Thomas Aquinas Catholic Church can be seen across the river.

University of Nevada students participating in World War II aircraft crew training at Sky Ranch in the Spanish Springs Valley north of Reno.

Cadets in the aircraft crew training program: Alex Mazur on the left and Robert W.
Anderson on the right, with their friend Andy, outside of the gym on campus.

The Washoe County Courthouse.

The 1946 Reno Rodeo parade, with a horse-drawn float sponsored by Harolds Club. The Washoe County Courthouse and the Riverside Hotel are in the background. An active "Harolds Club or Bust" international marketing campaign seemed to have worked. It was the largest casino in the world for 15 years. Howard Hughes bought it in 1970, after a period of decline.

The Mapes Hotel in July 1947, prior to its opening. The Mapes was the first skyscraper built in the Western United States after World War II. The art deco building was one of the first hotel-casino combinations.

The University of Nevada was a popular location for shooting college movies in the late 1940s, due to the Ivy League look of the campus and its proximity to California. This scene is from the filming of *Mother is a Freshman,* a 1949 movie starring Loretta Young, Van Johnson, and Rudy Vallee.

The Gay Nineties Review, a stage show in the Golden Hotel and Casino in 1948.

Governor Vail Pittman with members of the 565th Army Air Force Base Unit, 3rd Operational Training Unit, Ferrying Division, ATC, Reno Army Air Base (later the Stead Air Base) in 1948.

The Freedom Train stopping in Reno on March 22, 1948, on its 33,000-mile
journey to all 48 states, carrying 127 original manuscripts documenting U.S. history.

This north-facing view of Virginia Street shows a tethered blimp promoting Harolds Club and a banner for a Policeman's Ball (ca. 1949).

The Truckee River inundated Island Avenue, along with much of downtown, in November 1950.

GROWING AND THRIVING

(1950–1979)

Reno grew quickly after World War II. New interstate highways, improved air travel, a larger, more affluent, and more mobile population, and a robust national economy contributed to growth in tourism. The Winter Olympics at Squaw Valley in 1960, 50 miles from Reno, brought a new kind of international attention to the area and strengthened the city's infrastructure, especially the airport.

Gambling was too important to the economy to be further debated, but now Reno had competition from Las Vegas and from other states that were allowing gambling for the first time. In 1960, Las Vegas surpassed Reno in population, 64,405 to 51,270. The marriage business diminished as Las Vegas became "the place to go" for a quickie wedding, and the divorce business faded away as other states liberalized their laws. Gambling establishments finally broke out of the "red zone" area in which they had always been confined.

With Las Vegas on the scene, city leaders worked to develop a new image and reach out to new markets. A number of festivals brought specialized interest groups to the city, for whom gambling was of little or no interest. The first Basque festival in the U.S. was held in Sparks in 1959, becoming an annual tradition and spreading to other parts of the West. The annual Reno Air Races attracted international participants. The city also began to advertise itself as "Reno-Tahoe" to improve its image.

Meanwhile, most of Reno's population had no association with gambling or tourism. A growing need for housing, goods, and services provided ample jobs for newcomers. The University of Nevada grew quickly as the state's population swelled, and soldiers attending college on the G.I. Bill contributed to the university's development. In 1957 a new branch of the school opened in Las Vegas and became autonomous in 1968, ending the Reno campus' reign as the state's only university.

Reno's optimal location on transportation routes and its pro-business tax structure led to a new industry, warehousing. Returning to its origins, Reno grew as a distribution center, this time for goods arriving by sea in West Coast ports, destined for locations to the east.

Like any booming city, Reno has grappled with growth issues. Nevada political traditions support free enterprise, lack of regulation, and the right of individuals to make personal choices; thus, Reno organizations and businesses have continued to play developmental and social roles that governments would assume in other cities and states.

Sandbags at North Virginia and First streets in front of Woolworth's during the 1950 flood. There was little chance to prepare as the water rose quickly above the banks of the Truckee after four days of rain.

The 1950 flood was the worst on record, causing more than $6,000,000 of damage to downtown businesses. Hundreds of people helped move merchandise out of stores such as the Gray Reid Wright department store and Federal Outfitters. Automobiles were no match for the rushing water in the streets.

Another view of the 1950 flood, with the Majestic Theater in the background. Reno has survived devastating floods in 1907, 1928, 1937, 1955, 1963, 1964, 1986, 1997, and 2006.

In 1955, airmen such as this one were confined in small boxes at the counter-brainwashing school as part of their Cold War training at Stead Air Force Base. The base was established in Reno in 1942 to train signal companies for the war. It was given to the City of Reno in 1966, and then sold to Bill Lear in 1968. He worked on an unsuccessful low-pollution, steam-powered engine project.

Riders in the 1951 Fourth of July rodeo parade pass the Mystic Theater, which was showing a Western, appropriately enough. All Reno citizens were expected to wear Western attire during the rodeo week

Virginia Street near the river, with the Washoe County Courthouse, Riverside Hotel, and Mapes Hotel. Shirley Bassey, headlining at the Riverside, had her first hit in 1957 with *Banana Boat Song*. She would later record the theme songs for three James Bond movies.

Some of the celebrities in Reno in the early 1950s: Bing Crosby with Gorgeous George, a flamboyant wrestler-entertainer, who came to Reno for exhibition matches. Crosby, who owned a ranch in Elko County, Nevada, was a frequent visitor to Reno.

The New Hope Covenant Church in Sparks in the 1950s.

The Episcopal Church, originally at Second and Sierra, later moved to Eighth and University.

Steer wrestling at the Reno Rodeo in 1950. The first annual rodeo was held in 1919; for decades it was a Fourth of July event that included a downtown parade.

The Washoe Medical Center in 1957, one of Reno's two major hospitals.

The First Baptist Church interior during the "decommissioning service,"
January 19, 1956. The church was built in 1918 and sold in 1956.

Justice Charles M. Merrill of the Nevada Supreme Court swears in the new graduates at the 1956 commencement ceremony in the gymnasium of the University of Nevada in its last year as Nevada's lone university. The new Las Vegas branch first held classes in 1957 and eventually attained its autonomy in 1968. When that school became the University of Nevada, Las Vegas in 1969, the Reno institution lengthened its name to the University of Nevada, Reno.

Bill Harrah bought a small bingo parlor in Reno in 1937 and built it into a gambling empire. While most of his profits went into expanding the business, his passion for automobiles resulted in a collection of 1,400 classic vehicles, some of which are shown in this Sparks warehouse. After Harrah's death, most of the collection was sold, but 175 of his vintage autos became the basis for Reno's National Automobile Museum.

An aerial photo of Reno, April 1957, shows the Truckee River in the center.

Dan Blocker, who played Hoss Cartwright on television's *Bonanza,* with visitors on the set of the Ponderosa Ranch between Reno and Lake Tahoe in the 1960s. Episodes from the last five years of the show were filmed here. The Ponderosa was operated as a theme park from 1967 until 2004.

The Donner Trail Guest Ranch in Verdi, outside of Reno, was one of several temporary domiciles for divorce-seekers during the required residency in Nevada (three months, later reduced to six weeks). Some of the temporary residents stayed in hotels or rented homes and kept to themselves. Most guest ranches served a social purpose, maintaining a party atmosphere and offering organized outdoor activities such as horseback rides and hikes.

The Basque Sheepherder statue honors the Basques who first came to Nevada from France and Spain to herd sheep in the 1800s and continued that tradition into the 1970s. Once in Nevada, Basques frequently succeeded in ranching and other realms. The most prominent Basque Nevadan was Paul Laxalt, a governor and U.S. senator. His brother Robert wrote *Sweet Promised Land,* a powerful story of their father's emigration.

Following Spread: The Great Reno Balloon Race began in 1964 as part of the Air Races program but was discontinued after a couple of years. Revived in 1981, it is now held each September. Other transportation-themed festivals that draw large crowds are Hot August Nights for classic car enthusiasts, Street Vibrations (a gathering of motorcyclists), and the Reno Air Races in September.

Three men visit during a slow spell in Becker's Café, September 10, 1965.

The Reno skyline in the 1970s shows how far the former frontier town had come since Myron Lake built a hotel beside a river crossing during the 1860s silver rush.

NOTES ON THE PHOTOGRAPHS

These notes, listed by page number, attempt to include all aspects known of the photographs. Each of the photographs is identified by the page number, photograph's title or description, photographer and collection, archive, and call or box number when applicable. Although every attempt was made to collect all available data, in some cases complete data was unavailable due to the age and condition of some of the photographs and records.